Pet Goldfish

Cecelia H. Brannon

Enslow Publishing
101 W. 23rd Street
Suite 240
New York, NY 10011
USA

enslow.com

Published in 2017 by Enslow Publishing, LLC.
101 W. 23rd Street, Suite 240, New York, NY 10011

Library of Congress Cataloging-in-Publication Data
Names: Brannon, Cecelia H., author.
Title: Pet goldfish / Cecelia H. Brannon.
Description: New York, NY : Enslow Publishing, 2017. | Series: All about pets | Audience: Ages 6+. |
  Audience: K to grade 3. | Includes bibliographical references and index.
Identifiers: LCCN 2015045445| ISBN 9780766076068 (library bound) | ISBN 9780766076327 (pbk.) |
  ISBN 9780766075887 (6-pack)
Subjects: LCSH: Goldfish—Juvenile literature.
Classification: LCC SF458.G6 B73 2017 | DDC 639.3/7484—dc23
LC record available at http://lccn.loc.gov/2015045445

Printed in Malaysia

To Our Readers: We have done our best to make sure all website addresses in this book were active and appropriate when we went to press. However, the author and the publisher have no control over and assume no liability for the material available on those websites or on any websites they may link to. Any comments or suggestions can be sent by e-mail to customerservice@enslow.com.

Photos Credits: Cover, dien/Shutterstock.com; p. 1 pruit phatsrivong/Shutterstock.com; pp. 3 (left), 16 jirawatfoto/Shutterstock.com; pp. 3 (center), 14 dien/Shutterstock.com; pp. 3 (right), 6 Ingram Publishing/Thinkstock; pp. 4–5 AppStock/Shutterstock.com; p. 8 Jose Luis Pelaez Inc/Blend Images/ Thinkstock; p. 10 Comstock/Stockbyte/Thinkstock; p. 12 visa netpakdee/Shutterstock.com; p. 18 Zagorodnaya/Shutterstock.com; p. 20 smirart/iStock/Thinkstock; p. 22 Green Jo/Shutterstock.com.

Contents

Words to Know

fins   **scales**   **tank**

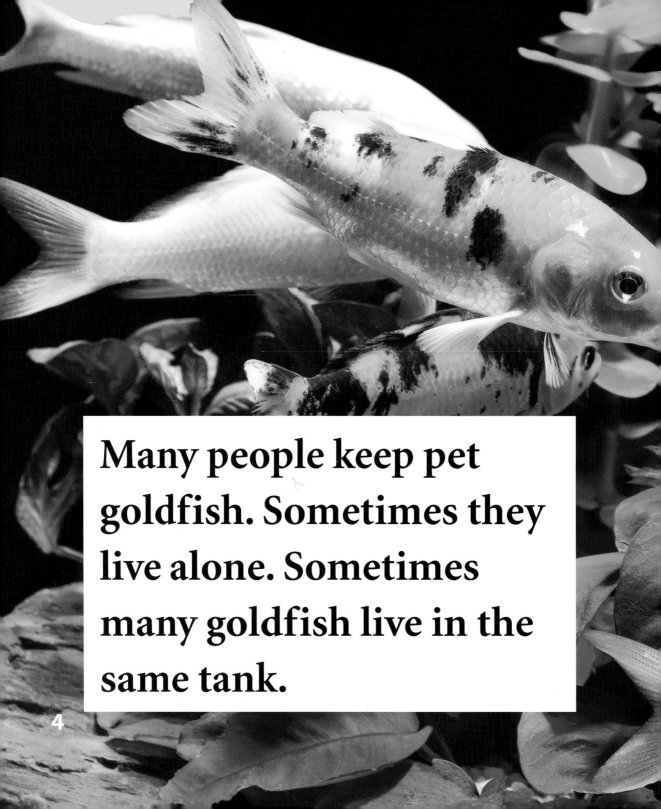

Many people keep pet goldfish. Sometimes they live alone. Sometimes many goldfish live in the same tank.

Goldfish must live in a bowl or tank with water. The tank should be large so that the goldfish has room to grow.

The bowl or tank must be cleaned every week. The goldfish must be out of the bowl before you clean it.

Goldfish eat fish food.
This is sprinkled on top of
the water.

Most goldfish are yellow or orange. But some have black or white scales, too!

A goldfish has seven fins. These help it swim all over its tank.

Goldfish do not sleep like people do. A goldfish keeps its eyes open when it sleeps.

Some people win goldfish as prizes at fairs. Others get their goldfish from a pet store.

Goldfish can be different sizes. Some can grow to be longer than this book!

If you take good care of your goldfish, it could live 30 years!

Read More

Ganeri, Anita. *Goldie's Guide to Caring for Your Goldfish*. Portsmouth, NH: Heinemann, 2013.

Hutmacher, Kimberly M. *I Want a Goldfish*. North Mankato, MN: Capstone Press, 2012.

Websites

Ducksters
duksters.com/animals/goldfish.php

Science Kids
sciencekids.co.nz/sciencefacts/animals/fish.html

Index

Guided Reading Level: B
Guided Reading Leveling System is based on the guidelines recommended by Fountas and Pinnell.

Word Count: 158